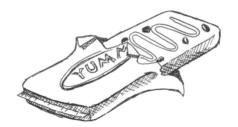

The Best 50
ENERGY BAR COOKIES

David Woods

BRISTOL PUBLISHING ENTERPRISES
Hayward, California

Printed in the United States of America.
ISBN: 1-55867-319-9

Cover design:	Frank J. Paredes
Cover photography:	John A. Benson
Food stylist:	Randy Mon
Illustration:	Nora Wylde

A SWEET, SIMPLE, PORTABLE ENERGY SNACK

Energy bars (also called sports bars, nutrition bars, breakfast bars, food bars, cereal bars and snack bars), developed as a source of fuel for athletes during exercise, have now have gone mainstream. Energy bars travel well, providing a ready source of energy without taking up much valuable packing space. They can be individually wrapped so they won't make a mess in your purse, briefcase, school locker or desk. Well wrapped, most will keep for weeks in the pantry or refrigerator.

The bars in this book provide a sweet taste, yet they typically contain more nutrients and less fat than candy bars. Most are made from a combination of grains; dried fruits or fruit fillings; sweeteners such as brown sugar, molasses or corn syrup; and other flavorful additions such as nuts, chocolate chips, marshmallows and spices.

Replenishing carbohydrates and fats that the body consumes during exercise can prevent you from burning out on a long workout. Just as you always drink water or sports drinks before and during exercise to replenish fluids, you should also replace the carbs and nutrients burned during exercise. Refuel your body with the good carbs, proteins, vitamins and minerals found in fruits, nuts, seeds and whole grains. And every body needs a small amount of fat to stay healthy. The key is to consume mono- or polyunsaturated fats, like those found in nuts, seeds and wheat germ.

Note, however, that energy bars alone will not make you stronger or faster, nor will they burn fat by themselves. They are not meant to replace a balanced diet and exercise plan. Consider them a supplement when your energy is running a little low.

SOME GREAT TIPS FOR BAKING BETTER BARS

- Never use diet or whipped margarine or any product labeled "lite" or "spread" in your bar cookies; the results will be disappointing.

- I prefer to use unsalted butter, but some like shortening; you may use half butter and half shortening, if you wish. Bars will be more moist if you use butter. If you do use shortening, you can add a teaspoon of water per cup of shortening.

MEASURE YOUR INGREDIENTS CAREFULLY

Clear glass or plastic measuring cups, usually with spouts, are good for measuring liquids. For dry ingredients, use measuring cups like the ones that comes as a "nested" set. Do not dip the measuring cup into the flour container; otherwise you will get a compacted measurement and too much flour. Instead, spoon flour from the container into the measuring cup and use a spatula or the flat side of a knife to level the flour even with the top of the cup.

Once flour is added to the ingredients, mix just enough to combine. Too much handling will develop the gluten in the flour, producing tough bars. Don't use an electric mixer to mix ingredients, unless specified by the recipe. Mix with a wooden spoon to avoid overmixing.

PREPARING THE PAN AND BAKING THE COOKIES

For best results, grease the pan with either nonstick cooking spray or shortening; or line the pan with waxed paper, parchment paper or aluminum foil. If butter or margarine are used, they can be absorbed into the batter — not a problem for bars that don't require baking. When using parchment paper, spray or lightly grease the baking pan. Cut paper to fit, place it in the pan, then lightly spray or grease the parchment. When using aluminum foil, turn the pan upside down and "mold" a piece of foil around the pan. Remove the foil "mold" from pan and turn pan right side up. Place the foil mold into the pan and lightly grease the aluminum foil with a nonstick cooking spray or shortening.

- A pan that is too large will result in a thin, dry bar. An under-sized pan will result in overcooked edges and a raw center.

- When baking with a nonstick cooking spray, be sure to wash the pans well. Otherwise, the residue left by the spray will become gummy, causing future baked goods to stick. When possible, use a light-colored aluminum, non-insulated baking pan; dark pans absorb more heat, which can result in burned bottoms and edges.

- Make sure to spread the batter evenly in the baking pan, so that the finished bars aren't thin and dried out in one corner and thick and underdone in another.

- Those of you who live at high altitude know that food cooks faster for you. You may need to reduce the oven temperature or baking time. Since bars continue to brown a little after removing from the oven, bake to a slightly lighter color than desired.

- When possible, bake one pan of bars at a time, placing it in the middle of the oven. If you must bake two pans at the same time, stagger them in the oven and rotate the pans from top to bottom and front to back halfway through the baking time.

CHECKING FOR DONENESS

Be sure to check your bar cookies at least 5 minutes before the minimum baking time has elapsed. Generally, bars are done when a wooden toothpick inserted in the center comes out clean or a moist — not wet — crumb is adhered to it.

TIPS FOR CUTTING YOUR BARS

First, always cool the pan completely on a wire rack before cutting; otherwise the bars will crumble and fall apart. After cooling and before cutting bars, place them in the freezer for just a few minutes to firm up; you'll have an easier time cutting them. If you flip the cooled bar out of the pan in one piece, you'll have an easier time cutting neat squares. This is easiest to do if your pan has been lined with paper or foil before baking.

Bars are usually cut into squares or rectangles with a sharp knife. They also can be cut into triangles or diamonds. For triangles, cut into 3-inch squares and then cut each square in half diagonally. To make diamonds, cut parallel lines 2 inches apart across the length of the pan and then cut diagonal lines 2 inches apart. Cookie cutters can be used to make different shapes. Kids especially love this.

FROSTING AND DECORATING YOUR BARS

Before serving, bars can be decorated or frosted right in their pans. Try drizzling each square with your favorite melted chocolate. For a more substantial coating, sprinkle the bars with butterscotch or chocolate chips right after they come out of the oven. Cover with foil and let set for about five minutes or until the chips melt. Use a rubber spatula to spread the melted topping. When cool, cut into bars. For bars made with fruits or nuts, make a simple icing of sifted confectioner's sugar mixed with enough freshly squeezed lemon or orange juice (plus a bit of grated zest) to achieve the desired consistency; drizzle over bars.

FRUIT AND COCONUT ENERGY BARS

Makes 16 bars

So crispy, chewy and moist! If you bike or hike, take these bars with you for a tasty boost of carbs and proteins.

1 cup soy nut butter
½ cup honey
½ cup light corn syrup
¼ tsp. vanilla extract
⅓ cup shelled chopped
   pumpkin seeds

½ cup chopped dried strawberries
½ cup chopped dried peaches
1 tbs. sesame seeds
⅓ cup shredded coconut
3 cups crispy rice cereal

Lightly butter an 8-inch square pan. In a large saucepan, stir together soy nut butter, honey, syrup and vanilla. Cook over low heat until mixture boils, stirring constantly. Remove from heat. Add pumpkin seeds, strawberries, peaches, sesame seeds and coconut and mix thoroughly. Add cereal and stir to coat. Press firmly into prepared pan. Cover and refrigerate for 2 hours. Cut into bars.

PUMPKIN ENERGY BARS

Makes 18 bars

Pumpkin, high in vitamin C and fiber, makes a moist bar.

1 can (15 oz.) pumpkin puree
1/2 cup egg whites (3-4)
3/4 cup unsweetened applesauce
3/4 cup packed light brown
  sugar
1 1/4 cups whole wheat flour

1/2 cup old-fashioned oats
1/4 cup wheat germ
1 tbs. pumpkin pie spice
1/2 tsp. baking soda
1 cup dried cranberries
1/2 cup chopped walnuts

Heat oven to 350°. Spray a 9 x 13-inch pan with nonstick cooking spray. In large bowl, thoroughly mix pumpkin, egg whites, applesauce and brown sugar. Stir in flour, oats, wheat germ, spice, baking soda, cranberries and walnuts. Mix well for 2 minutes. Pour into prepared pan. Bake for 35 to 40 minutes, or until a toothpick inserted in the center comes out clean. Cool completely on a wire rack. Cut into bars.

SOY OAT ENERGY BARS

Makes 24 bars

These bars are high fiber and protein and sweetened with honey.

3 cups old-fashioned oats
1 cup vanilla soy protein
1 cup whole wheat flour
1/2 cup each chopped, dried
    mango and pineapple
1/2 cup unsalted soy nuts

1 tsp. baking powder
1/2 tsp. cinnamon
3/4 tsp. ground cardamom
1/2 cup honey
1/4 cup soy oil or canola oil
1/2 cup applesauce

Heat oven to 350°. Lightly grease a 9-inch square pan. In a food processor workbowl, combine oats, soy protein, flour, mango, pineapple, soy nuts, baking powder, cinnamon and cardamom. Pulse a few times to chop. Add honey, oil and applesauce. Process for 10 seconds. If necessary, add a few tbs. water to make a stiff dough, and process a few seconds. Press dough evenly into prepared pan. Bake for 10 to 15 minutes, until golden brown. Cool on a wire rack. Cut into bars.

CRANBERRY NUT ENERGY BARS

Makes 24 bars

Try using peanut butter or tahini instead of soy nut butter.

2 cups quick-cooking oats
2 cups dried cranberries
2½ cups crispy rice cereal
1 cup chopped soy nuts
½ cup shredded coconut

½ cup chopped dried
   strawberries
½ cup margarine
½ cup soy nut butter
1 bag (10½ oz.) marshmallows

Heat oven to 350°. Spread oats on a 9 x 13-inch pan. Bake, stirring occasionally, for about 15 minutes, until oats are toasted. Set aside oats. Lightly spray the 9 x 13-inch pan with nonstick cooking spray. In a large bowl, combine cranberries, cereal, soy nuts, coconut, strawberries and oats. In a large saucepan, melt margarine, soy nut butter and marshmallows over low heat, stirring occasionally. Add oats mixture and stir to coat. Press mixture firmly into prepared pan. Cool completely and cut into bars.

ENERGY SURVIVAL BARS

Makes 24 bars

All the dried fruit and crispy goodness makes these bars great for maintaining a steady supply of energy. Take them hiking anytime.

½ cup sesame seeds	½ cup dried apricots
3 cups crispy rice cereal	¼ cup orange juice
1 cup chopped almonds	½ cup peanut butter
1 cup prunes	¼ cup maple syrup
1 cup dried peaches	½ tsp. ground ginger
½ cup dried apples	

Line a 9-inch square pan with waxed paper. In a large bowl, combine sesame seeds, cereal and almonds. Set aside. In a food processor workbowl, combine prunes, peaches, apples, apricots, orange juice, peanut butter, syrup and ginger. Process until smooth, scraping down the sides a few times. Combine mixtures. Mix thoroughly. Press into prepared pan. Let air-dry overnight. Cut into bars.

HAWAIIAN TROPICAL ENERGY BARS

Makes 16 bars

These are a fantastic chewy and fruity treat—kids love them too.

¼ cup chopped walnuts
½ cup dried cranberries
½ cup each chopped, dried papaya, mango, star fruit and pineapple
½ cup unsweetened shredded coconut

½ tsp. ground cardamom
1 cup whole wheat flour
3 tbs. vegetable oil
1 tsp. vanilla extract
2 eggs
1 egg white
¾ cup mango or apricot nectar

Heat oven to 350°. Spray an 8-inch square pan with nonstick cooking spray. In a large bowl, combine walnuts, dried fruits, coconut, cardamom and flour. Mix well. In a medium bowl, mix together oil, vanilla, eggs, egg white and nectar until well combined. Add liquid mixture to flour mixture and mix well. Spread evenly into prepared pan. Bake for 1 hour, or until a toothpick inserted in the center comes out clean. Cool on a wire rack. Cut into bars.

POWER BARS

Feel free to substitute any of your favorite dried fruits or nuts in these energy-packed bars. If you don't have a standing mixer, use a hand-held mixer to cream the butter, sweeteners and egg until light. Then stir in the remaining ingredients by hand.

1 cup quick-cooking oats
1/2 cup sliced almonds
1/2 cup raisins
1/2 cup pitted chopped dates
1/2 cup chopped dried apricots
1/3 cup unsalted butter, softened
1/2 cup packed brown sugar
1/4 cup light molasses
1 egg

1 cup all-purpose flour
1/4 cup whole wheat flour
1/2 cup nonfat dry milk powder
1/4 cup toasted wheat germ
1 1/2 tsp. baking powder
1/2 tsp. baking soda
1/2 tsp. vanilla extract
1/2 cup soymilk

Heat oven to 300°. Place oats and almonds in an ungreased 9 x 13-inch pan. Toast in oven for 10 minutes. Set oat mixture aside to cool slightly. Grease the 9 x 13-inch pan. Turn oven to 325°.

Combine raisins, dates, apricots, oats and almonds in a food processor workbowl. Pulse about 10 times, until coarsely chopped. Set aside.

In the bowl of a heavy-duty mixer fitted with a paddle, beat butter, brown sugar, molasses and egg until light and fluffy.

In a separate bowl, combine flours, dry milk, wheat germ, baking powder and baking soda.

Mix into creamed mixture. Add vanilla and soymilk and mix thoroughly. Stir in reserved dried fruit mixture. Spread batter evenly in prepared pan. Bake for 30 minutes, or until set. Cool completely on a wire rack. Cut into bars.

RAISIN ENERGY SNACK BARS

Makes 48 bars

Pack these little bars in small plastic bags for on-the-go energy.

4 egg whites
¼ cup sugar
4 tsp. vegetable oil
1 tsp. cinnamon
¾ tsp. vanilla extract
1⅔ cups low-fat granola

1 cup raisins
3 tbs. toasted wheat germ
3 tbs. raw shelled sunflower
  seeds
4 tsp. sesame seeds

Heat oven to 300°. Coat a 9 x 13-inch pan with nonstick cooking spray. In a large bowl, beat egg whites and sugar with a whisk until smooth. Beat in oil, cinnamon and vanilla. Stir in granola, raisins, wheat germ, sunflower seeds and sesame seeds; blend well. Press mixture into prepared pan. Bake for 20 to 25 minutes, until golden brown. Cool for 5 minutes in pan. Loosen edges with a spatula and invert onto a wire rack to cool completely before cutting.

BLUEBERRY ENERGY BARS

Makes 32 bars

Blueberries are packed with vitamin C and fiber; apricots have calcium and potassium. Kids love making these bars.

1 cup dried blueberries	peanut butter
2 cups each pitted dates, dried	1/2 cup shelled sunflower seeds
apples, prunes, dried apricots	8 cups old-fashioned oats
1 cup raisins	1 1/2 cups dry pancake mix
1 jar (8 oz.) almond paste or	2 cups honey

Heat oven to 375°. Dice all of the fruits to same size as raisins. Place fruit and almond paste in a large bowl; knead to combine. Add sunflower seeds, oats and pancake mix and knead. Add honey and knead until all is mixed well.

Press mixture onto a cookie sheet to 3/8- to 1/2-inch thick, and as even as possible. Bake for 20 minutes, or until top is light brown. Cool completely on a wire rack before cutting into bars.

DATE ENERGY BARS

Makes 12 bars

Children love dates because they're high in natural sugar, but they're also high in vitamin B and minerals. These tasty bars are also surprisingly low in fat.

1/3 cup honey
1/4 cup orange juice
2 tbs. plus 1 tsp. lemon juice, divided
24 pitted dates, chopped
2 1/2 cups whole wheat flour
1/2 tsp. baking soda
1/4 tsp. baking powder
1/4 cup maple syrup
2 egg whites
1 tbs. vegetable oil

Heat oven to 350°. Lightly coat a 9 x 13-inch pan with nonstick cooking spray. In a small bowl mix honey, orange juice and 2 tbs. of the lemon juice. Stir in dates.

In a large bowl combine flour, baking soda and baking powder. In a small bowl mix maple syrup, egg whites, oil and remaining 1 tsp. lemon juice. Add to flour mixture. Beat with an electric mixer or by hand until combined, scraping sides of bowl frequently (mixture will be crumbly).

Add date mixture and beat until combined. Spread batter in prepared pan. Bake for 12 to 15 minutes, or until top is light golden and a toothpick inserted in the center comes out clean. Cool in pan on a wire rack. Cut into bars.

FRUIT AND OATS ENERGY BARS

Makes 15 bars

Oats are easily digested, high in fiber, and help lower cholesterol.

3 cups old-fashioned oats
1/2 cup shelled chopped
  pumpkin seeds
1/2 cup chopped hazelnuts
3/4 cup margarine, softened
1/2 cup packed brown sugar

1/2 cup honey
1/2 tsp. ground ginger
1/4 tsp. ground cloves
1/2 cup each chopped, dried
  banana chips, peaches, and
  star fruit

Heat oven to 350°. Combine oats, pumpkin seeds and hazelnuts in a 10 x 15-inch pan. Bake for 15 to 20 minutes, stirring occasionally, until seeds and nuts begin to brown. Set aside. Butter and flour the 10 x 15-inch pan. In a large saucepan over low heat, melt margarine. Remove from heat and add brown sugar, honey, ginger and cloves. Stir in oats mixture and dried fruits until a stiff dough forms. Press firmly into prepared pan in an even layer. Bake for 20 to 25 minutes, until browned. Cool on a wire rack. Cut into bars.

FRUIT AND NUT BREAKFAST BARS

Makes 24 bars

High in potassium and vitamins A and C, mangos have a delicious citrus flavor. You could also use dried apricots in this recipe.

1 cup chopped golden raisins	1/2 cup packed brown sugar
1/2 cup chopped dried mango	2 eggs
1 tbs. flour	1/3 cup margarine, melted
1 1/4 cups oats	1/2 tsp. vanilla extract
1/2 cup chopped almonds	1/8 tsp. almond extract

Heat oven to 350°. Spray a 9 x 13-inch pan with nonstick cooking spray. In a large bowl, combine raisins, mango and flour. Add oats, almonds and brown sugar and stir to combine. In a small bowl stir together eggs, margarine, vanilla and almond extract; mix well. Add to oat mixture and stir until moistened. Press mixture into prepared pan. Bake for 25 minutes, or until golden brown. Place on a wire rack to cool completely. Cut into bars.

BREAKFAST ENERGY BARS

Makes 16 bars

These are filled with vitamin and mineral nourishment from bananas, wheat germ and dried fruit.

2 medium bananas, mashed
1/4 cup honey
1/2 cup molasses
1 tbs. cornstarch
1 tsp. vanilla extract
1/4 cup water
1/2 cup applesauce
1/2 cup wheat germ
1/2 cup whole wheat flour

1 tsp. cinnamon
1/2 tsp. ground cardamom
1/2 tsp. baking soda
1/2 cup each chopped dried strawberries, peaches, apricots and star fruit
1 cup sweetened shredded coconut
3 cups quick-cooking oats

Heat oven to 350°. Lightly spray an 8-inch square pan with non-stick cooking spray.

In a large bowl, thoroughly combine bananas, honey, molasses, cornstarch, vanilla, water and applesauce. Stir in wheat germ, flour, cinnamon, cardamom, baking soda, strawberries, peaches, apricots, star fruit and coconut. Mix well. Mix in oats. Dough will be heavy and grainy.

Press dough firmly into prepared pan. Bake for 15 to 20 minutes, or until lightly browned. Cool completely on a wire rack. Cut into bars.

APPLE BREAKFAST BARS

Makes 12 bars

Fiber-rich apples add moisture and richness without the fat, and boost your levels of vitamins A and C.

½ cup whole wheat flour
½ cup all-purpose flour
1 cup old-fashioned oats
½ cup packed brown sugar
¼ tsp. baking soda
1½ tsp. apple pie spice

1½ cups grated apples
1 egg
⅓ cup light corn syrup
2 tbs. vegetable oil
½ cup raisins or currants
½ cup chopped walnuts

Heat oven to 350°. Spray a 9-inch square pan with nonstick cooking spray. In a bowl, combine flours, oats, brown sugar, baking soda and spice. Add apples, egg, syrup, oil, raisins and walnuts, mixing until combined. Spread evenly in prepared pan. Bake for 25 minutes, or until light golden brown and a toothpick inserted in center comes out clean. Cool completely on a wire rack. Cut into bars.

CHEERIOS BREAKFAST BARS

Makes 12-24 bars

A portable version of a bowl of cereal gets a protein boost from peanut butter and powdered milk.

$^1/_2$ cup margarine
32 large marshmallows, or 3 cups mini marshmallows
$^1/_2$ cup peanut butter
$^1/_2$ cup nonfat dry milk powder
1 cup raisins
3 cups Cheerios

Grease a 9-inch square pan. In a large saucepan, melt margarine and marshmallows over low heat, stirring constantly. Stir in peanut butter until melted. Stir in dry milk.

Remove from heat. Stir in raisins and cereal until evenly coated. Pat cereal mixture evenly into prepared pan. Refrigerate until firm. Cut into bars.

FRUITY CEREAL BARS

Makes 16 bars

Try any combination of dried fruits in this recipe: apricots, cherries, cranberries, mango, papaya, peaches, pears, blueberries, pineapple, raisins, star fruit and strawberries are a few suggestions.

1 box (14 oz.) low-fat granola with raisins
1½ cups mini marshmallows
½ cup apricot preserves
6 tbs. (¾ stick) butter or margarine
¼ cup packed dark brown sugar
1⅓ cups diced mixed dried fruit

Spray an 8-inch square pan with nonstick cooking spray. Line bottom of pan with waxed paper cut to fit. Coat paper with nonstick cooking spray. Put granola in a heavy-gauge plastic bag and crush finely with a rolling pin or the bottom of a heavy pan; set aside.

In a large nonstick saucepan over medium-low heat, stir marshmallows, preserves, butter and brown sugar until marshmallows melt and mixture is smooth. Remove from heat. Stir in granola and dried fruit until well coated.

Press into prepared pan and cover with waxed paper. Place another 8-inch square pan or heavy book on top. Press to compact mixture into an even, firm layer. Refrigerate until firm, about 1½ hours. Invert onto a cutting board and remove waxed paper. Cut into bars. Store loosely covered at room temperature for up to 1 week.

WHEAT GERM BREAKFAST BARS

Makes 9 bars

Wheat germ is a major source of vitamin E, and has a nutty flavor and crunchy texture. Toast the wheat germ in a dry skillet over medium heat for a few minutes to bring out the flavor.

¾ cup all-purpose flour
¾ cup toasted wheat germ
¼ cup sugar
½ tsp. baking powder
½ tsp. cinnamon
¼ cup (½ stick) butter, softened

¼ cup honey
1 egg
½ tsp. vanilla extract
1 cup raisins
½ cup chopped walnuts

Heat oven to 350°. Grease an 8-inch square pan. In a large bowl combine flour, wheat germ, sugar, baking powder and cinnamon. Stir in butter, honey, egg and vanilla; mix well. Stir in raisins and walnuts. Press mixture firmly into prepared pan. Bake for 20 to 25 minutes, or until lightly browned.

CHEERIOS-PAPAYA ENERGY BARS

Makes 24 bars

The easy digestibility of these bars comes from the papaya.

1½ cups all-purpose flour
1 tsp. baking soda
1 tsp. cinnamon
¼ tsp. ground nutmeg
½ cup chopped dried papaya
1 egg

¾ cup sugar
1 cup applesauce
½ cup water
1 tbs. buttermilk
2 cups Cheerios, divided

Heat oven to 350°. Spray a 9 x 13-inch pan with nonstick cooking spray. In a bowl, combine flour, baking soda, cinnamon and nutmeg. Stir in papaya. In a large bowl, using a mixer, beat egg and sugar on high speed for 1 minute. Beat in applesauce. Alternately beat in flour mixture with water and buttermilk. Stir in 1½ cups of the cereal. Pour batter into prepared pan. Sprinkle top with remaining cereal. Bake for 15 minutes. Cool on a wire rack before cutting.

CRISPY RICE PEANUT BUTTER BARS

Makes 24 bars

These crunchy, sweet energy bars are just the thing to feed the kids after sporting events.

1 bag (10½ oz.) mini marshmallows
¼ cup (½ stick) margarine
1 cup dried cranberries
5 cups crispy rice cereal
2 tbs. peanut butter

Grease a 9 x 13-inch pan and set aside. In a large microwave-safe bowl, place marshmallows and margarine. Microwave on high for 3 minutes, until melted. Stir well.

Stir in peanut butter until well combined. Add cranberries and cereal, stirring to coating well. Press mixture into prepared pan. Cool for 10 minutes before cutting into bars.

PAPAYA BANANA ENERGY BARS

Makes 16 bars

These bars are loaded with minerals, folic acid and vitamins.

2 cups quick-cooking oats
1 cup chopped walnuts
1/3 cup butter
1/2 cup packed brown sugar
1/4 cup honey

1 cup diced dried papaya
1 cup dried banana chips
1 cup honey graham cereal
    squares

Heat oven to 350°. In an 8-inch square pan, combine oats and walnuts. Bake for 20 minutes, or until golden brown, stirring occasionally. Set aside. Lightly butter the 8-inch square pan. Combine butter, brown sugar and honey in a small saucepan. Cook over medium heat until mixture boils, stirring constantly. Remove from heat. In a bowl, mix papaya, banana chips and cereal. Add oats and walnuts. Combine mixtures and toss to coat thoroughly. Press firmly and evenly into prepared pan. Cool completely. Cut into 2-inch bars.

ORANGE ENERGY BARS

Makes 24 bars

Dried peaches will replace the potassium lost during exercise.

1 can (16 oz.) frozen orange juice concentrate, thawed, undiluted
1/2 cup chopped dried peaches
1/2 cup chopped dried mango
1/4 cup chopped hazelnuts
1 1/2 cups all-purpose flour
1 cup old-fashioned oats
1 tsp. baking powder
1/4 tsp. baking soda
1/2 cup (1 stick) butter, softened
1/2 cup packed brown sugar
1 egg
1 tsp. vanilla extract
1 tsp. grated orange zest

Heat oven to 350°. Grease a 9-inch square pan. In a medium saucepan, combine orange juice concentrate, peaches and mango. Cook over low heat, stirring occasionally, until mixture thickens, about 5 minutes. Remove from heat. Stir in hazelnuts and set aside.

In a large bowl combine flour, oats, baking powder and baking soda.

In a separate bowl beat together butter, brown sugar, egg, vanilla and orange zest until light and fluffy. Stir in dry mixture until blended. Press 2/3 of the dough into prepared pan. Spread reserved fruit mixture evenly over dough. Sprinkle remaining dough over fruit to form a crumb topping.

Bake for 30 to 35 minutes or until golden brown. Cool completely on a wire rack. Cut into bars.

QUICK ENERGY HIKER'S BARS

Dried pineapple is a healthy, sweet treat on its own, and is delicious in these bars.

½ cup chopped dried papaya
½ cup chopped dried pineapple
½ cup chopped dried strawberries
½ cup packed brown sugar
½ cup honey
1½ cups peanut butter
½ cup wheat germ
4½ cups Grape Nuts Flakes cereal

Grease an 11 x 7-inch pan. In a medium bowl, combine papaya, pineapple and strawberries. Set aside. In a large saucepan over medium heat, stir together brown sugar and honey. Bring to a boil, stirring constantly. Remove from heat. Stir in peanut butter until smooth. Stir in wheat germ and cereal. Set aside ⅓ cup of the dried fruit and stir remaining fruit into mixture. Spread mixture into prepared pan. Press reserved fruit into top. Cool. Cut into bars.

MANGO ALMOND ENERGY BARS

Makes 12 bars

These bars are quick to make and a snap to take along on a hike. They are a good source of potassium and beta carotene.

1½ cups quick-cooking oats
½ cup all-purpose flour
½ cup packed brown sugar
½ cup chopped dried mango
¼ cup golden raisins

⅓ cup toasted slivered almonds
¼ cup toasted wheat germ
1 egg
¼ cup vegetable oil
¼ cup corn syrup

Heat oven to 350°. In a large bowl, combine oats, flour, brown sugar, mango, raisins, almonds and wheat germ.

In a small bowl, beat together egg, oil and syrup. Stir into oats mixture until well combined.

Press firmly into an ungreased 9-inch square pan. Bake for 18 to 20 minutes, or until lightly browned. Cool on a wire rack. Cut into bars.

IRON ENERGY BARS

Makes 24 bars

Here's a delicious power bar that really gives you a boost of energy. It is protein-rich and provides essential vitamins and, thanks to the raisins and molasses, iron.

1 cup dried cranberries
½ cup golden raisins
⅓ cup margarine, softened
½ cup sugar
1 egg
½ cup light molasses
1¼ cups whole wheat flour
¼ cup toasted wheat germ

½ cup nonfat dry milk powder
½ tsp. baking soda
1½ tsp. baking powder
½ tsp. ground ginger
¼ tsp. ground cardamom
½ cup skim milk
1 cup shelled sunflower seeds
1 cup quick-cooking oats

Heat oven to 350°. Grease a 9 x 13-inch pan. Chop dried cranberries and raisins (using a food processor if possible).

In a large bowl beat together margarine, sugar, egg and molasses until creamy.

In a medium bowl combine flour, wheat germ, dry milk, baking soda, baking powder, ginger and cardamom. Stir into creamed mixture along with skim milk.

Stir in cranberry mixture, sunflower seeds and oats. Spread evenly into prepared pan. Bake for 30 minutes, or until golden. Cool completely on a wire rack. Cut into bars.

BANANA TRAIL MIX ENERGY BARS

Makes 16 bars

Bananas and applesauce add moistness as well as essential minerals to these low-fat bars.

2 medium bananas, mashed
1/4 cup honey
1/2 cup molasses
1 tbs. cornstarch
1 tsp. vanilla extract
1/2 cup applesauce
1/4 cup water
1 cup whole wheat flour
1 tsp. cinnamon
1/2 tsp. ground cloves
1/2 tsp. baking soda

1/2 cup dried cranberries
1/2 cup finely chopped dried papaya
1/2 cup chopped dried strawberries
1/2 cup chopped pecans
1/2 cup shelled sunflower seeds
1/2 cup chopped hazelnuts
3 cups quick-cooking oats

Heat oven to 350°. Lightly spray an 8-inch square pan with non-stick cooking spray.

In a large bowl thoroughly mix bananas, honey, molasses, cornstarch, vanilla, applesauce and water. Stir in flour, cinnamon, cloves and baking soda. Add dried cranberries, papaya, strawberries, pecans, sunflower seeds, hazelnuts and oats; stir to combine well.

Press dough into prepared pan. Bake for 12 to 15 minutes. Cool on a wire rack. Cut into bars.

PINEAPPLE-PAPAYA ENERGY BARS

Makes 36 bars

Use apricot nectar, found in your supermarket's juice aisle, if you can't find papaya nectar. Both are high in vitamin C.

1/4 cup chopped walnuts
1 cup dried cranberries
1/2 cup chopped dried papaya
1/2 cup chopped dried mango
1 cup finely chopped dried
   pineapple
1 tsp. minced crystallized ginger

1 cup whole wheat flour
3 tbs. canola oil
1 tsp. coconut extract
2 eggs
1 egg white
1/2 cup papaya nectar

Heat oven to 350°. Toast walnuts in a 9-inch square pan until golden brown, about 8 minutes. Set walnuts aside, and spray the 9-inch square pan with nonstick cooking spray.

In a large bowl combine toasted walnuts, dried cranberries, papaya, mango, pineapple, ginger and flour. Mix well.

In another bowl combine oil, coconut extract, eggs, egg white and nectar; mix well. Add liquid mixture to flour mixture and stir until just combined.

Spread evenly into prepared pan. Bake for 1 hour, or until a toothpick inserted in the center comes out clean. Cool completely on a wire rack. Cut into bars.

HONEY TRAIL MIX BARS

Makes 24 bars

The tangy-sweet, ridged carambola is usually called star fruit because it slices into perfect star shapes. Use any other dried fruit you like to substitute if you can't find dried star fruit.

3 1/2 cups old-fashioned oats
1 cup all-purpose flour
1 tsp. baking soda
1/2 tsp. ground cardamom
1 tsp. vanilla extract
2/3 cup butter, softened
1/2 cup honey
1/3 cup packed brown sugar

1/2 cup chopped dried
  strawberries
1/2 cup chopped dried cherries
1/2 cup dried cranberries
1/2 cup chopped dried star fruit
1/2 cup chopped hazelnuts
1/2 cup shredded coconut

Heat oven to 325°. Lightly grease a 9 x 13-inch pan.

In a large bowl combine oats, flour, baking soda and cardamom. Add vanilla, butter, honey and brown sugar. Beat with an electric mixer or by hand until smooth. Batter will be very stiff.

Using a wooden spoon, stir in strawberries, cherries, dried cranberries, star fruit, hazelnuts and coconut until well combined.

Press dough into prepared pan. Bake for 20 to 25 minutes, until golden brown. Cool completely on a wire rack. Cut into bars.

CHERRY ENERGY BARS

Tangy, chewy dried cherries are high in iron , vitamin C and fiber.

1 cup dried cherries
¼ cup apple juice
2 tsp. vanilla extract
¼ cup (½ stick) butter
2¼ cups old-fashioned oats
1 cup chopped hazelnuts
1 tsp. ground allspice
2 eggs, lightly beaten
⅓ cup honey

Heat oven to 350°. Lightly butter an 8-inch square pan.

In a medium bowl, mix cherries, apple juice and vanilla. Set aside for 20 minutes to allow cherries to plump.

While cherries soak, melt butter in a large skillet over medium heat. Add oats and hazelnuts and sauté, stirring constantly, for 3 to 4 minutes, until aromatic and toasted. Stir in allspice and cook for 1 minute.

Pour into a large bowl. Stir eggs and honey into reserved cherry mixture. Pour cherry mixture into oats mixture and stir until well blended.

Spread evenly into prepared pan. Bake for 30 minutes or until golden. Cool on a wire rack. Cut into bars.

LOW-FAT FITNESS ENERGY BARS

Sesame seeds and peanut butter provide a small amount of unsaturated fat in these healthy bars. Find protein powder in health food stores, or the natural foods section of your grocery store.

1½ cups old-fashioned oats
1 cup crispy rice cereal
¼ cup sesame seeds
1½ cups chopped dried papaya
1½ cups chopped dried
  pineapple
½ cup nonfat protein powder

½ cup toasted wheat germ
1 cup light corn syrup
½ cup sugar
½ cup peanut butter
1½ tsp. vanilla extract
½ tsp. cinnamon

Heat oven to 350°. Spread oats, cereal and sesame seeds in a 9 x 13-inch nonstick pan. Bake, stirring occasionally, until oats are toasted, about 15 minutes. Set aside oats mixture.

Lightly spray the 9 x 13-inch pan with cooking spray. In a large bowl mix together papaya, pineapple, protein powder, wheat germ and oats mixture.

In a heavy saucepan over medium heat, combine syrup and sugar; bring to a boil. Reduce heat to low and stir in peanut butter, vanilla and cinnamon. Quickly pour hot syrup mixture over oats mixture and stir well.

With a spatula immediately spread warm mixture into prepared pan, pressing into an even thin layer. (Caution: if you work too slowly, the mixture will harden and be difficult to spread.) Refrigerate until firm, at least 4 hours. Cut into bars.

STRAWBERRY ENERGY BARS

Makes 48 bars

Kids as well as adults will love these bars. Strawberries are very high in vitamin C and fiber, and also contain potassium. Look for protein powder in the natural foods section of your grocery store, or in health food stores.

2 cups chopped dried
   strawberries
²/₃ cup orange juice
¹/₂ cup chopped pecans
³/₄ cup margarine, softened
³/₄ cup packed brown sugar
¹/₄ cup honey

1 egg
1 cup all-purpose flour
1¹/₂ cups old-fashioned oats
¹/₂ cup nonfat protein powder
¹/₄ cup wheat germ
1 tsp. baking soda

Heat oven to 350°. Grease a 9 x 13-inch pan. Combine strawberries with orange juice in a blender container. Blend until almost smooth, scraping down the sides of the container a few times. Stir in pecans; set aside.

In a large bowl beat together margarine, brown sugar and honey until creamy. Beat in egg. Stir in flour, oats, protein powder, wheat germ and baking soda to blend thoroughly.

Spread a little less than half of the oat mixture evenly into prepared pan. Spread strawberry mixture evenly over flour mixture in pan, keeping the strawberry mixture to within ½ inch of the edges. Crumble remaining flour mixture over the top to cover the strawberry mixture and form a crumb topping. Pat down gently.

Bake for 30 to 35 minutes or until browned. Cool completely on a wire rack. Cut into bars.

TOASTED OATS AND FRUIT ENERGY BARS

Makes 15 bars

Oats, seeds and dried fruit combine for delicious nutrition. Toasting the oats, wheat germ, sesame seeds and almonds intensifies the flavor.

3 cups old-fashioned oats
1/2 cup wheat germ
1/2 cup sesame seeds
1/2 cup chopped almonds
3/4 cup margarine
1/2 cup honey

1/2 cup packed brown sugar
1/2 tsp. ground nutmeg
1/2 cup chopped dried cherries
1/2 cup chopped dried mango
1/2 cup sweetened shredded coconut

Heat oven to 350°. Combine oats, wheat germ, sesame seeds and almonds in a 10 x 15-inch jelly roll pan. Bake for 20 minutes, stirring occasionally, until nuts begin to brown.

Set oats mixture aside; butter and flour the 10 x 15-inch pan. In a large saucepan over medium heat, mix together margarine, honey and brown sugar. Add nutmeg and bring to a boil, stirring occasionally. Remove from heat and stir in toasted oat mixture, cherries, mango and coconut.

Press dough firmly into prepared pan in an even layer. Bake for 20 to 25 minutes, or until browned. Cool completely on a wire rack. Cut into 2 x 5-inch bars.

HEALTHY BREAKFAST ENERGY BARS

Makes 8-10 bars

Take your oatmeal on the go with these delicious bars. Protein powder can be found in health food stores.

1½ cups old-fashioned oats
½ cup whole wheat flour
½ cup nonfat protein powder
½ cup shredded coconut
½ cup chopped almonds

½ cup chopped dried papaya
½ cup honey
½ cup margarine, softened
1 egg, lightly beaten

Heat oven to 350°. Line an 8-inch square pan with parchment paper. In a bowl, mix oats, flour, protein powder, coconut, almonds and papaya. In a small saucepan, bring honey and margarine to a boil over medium heat, stirring frequently. Boil for 1 minute, stirring constantly. Cool slightly, then whisk in egg. Combine liquid and dry ingredients and mix well. Spread mixture in pan and bake for 25 minutes. Cut into bars while still warm. Cool and store in an airtight container.

CHEWY GRAPE NUTS ENERGY BARS

Make 24 bars

Protein powder can be found in natural foods stores.

1 cup quick-cooking oats
¼ cup all-purpose flour
¼ cup protein powder
½ cup Grape Nuts cereal
½ tsp. ground ginger
1 egg, lightly beaten
⅓ cup applesauce

¼ cup honey
¼ cup packed brown sugar
2 tbs. vegetable oil
2 cups chopped dried papaya
¼ cup shelled sunflower seeds
¼ cup chopped pecans

Heat oven to 325°. Line an 8-inch square pan with foil. Spray foil with nonstick spray. In a large bowl, combine oats, flour, protein powder, cereal and ginger. Add egg, applesauce, honey, brown sugar and oil. Mix well. Stir in papaya, sunflower seeds and pecans. Spread mixture evenly in prepared pan. Bake for 30 to 35 minutes, or until lightly browned around edges. Cool completely on a wire rack. Use edges of foil to lift from pan. Cut into bars.

MAPLE SYRUP PROTEIN BARS

Makes 18 bars

Soy nut butter and protein powder can be found in the natural foods section of most grocery stores. These bars will keep longer if refrigerated.

2 cups pure maple syrup
1 tbs. honey
2 cups soy nut butter
2 tbs. unsweetened cocoa
  powder

1/2 tsp. ground cardamom
1 1/2 cups protein powder
2 1/2 cups oats, ground in a food
  processor
1/2 cup chopped roasted soy nuts

Spray a 9-inch square pan with nonstick cooking spray. In a large bowl, mix maple syrup, honey, soy nut butter, cocoa powder and cardamom. Stir in protein powder until mixture becomes too stiff, and then use your hands to mix. Knead in oats and soy nuts. Dough will be very stiff. Spread dough evenly into prepared pan. Refrigerate for at least 1 hour. Cut into bars.

SESAME ENERGY BARS

Makes 24 bars

A combination of seeds and dried cranberries makes a tasty bar. If you don't have tahini, you can use another ½ cup of peanut butter.

½ cup peanut butter
½ cup tahini (sesame paste)
1 cup maple syrup
½ cup nonfat protein powder
1 cup sesame seeds
1 cup shelled sunflower seeds
½ cup dried cranberries

½ cup chopped pecans
½ cup sliced almonds
¼ cup shelled chopped
   pumpkin seeds
½ cup shredded unsweetened
   coconut

Spray a 9 x 13-inch pan with nonstick cooking spray. In a large saucepan, mix together peanut butter and tahini until blended. Add maple syrup and bring to a boil over medium heat, stirring occasionally. Add remaining ingredients and mix thoroughly. Spread evenly into prepared pan. Refrigerate until firm and cut into bars.

CAMPING BARS

Almonds contain a relatively small amount of unsaturated fat, and large amounts of potassium, magnesium, vitamin B, calcium and protein.

1/2 cup all-purpose flour
1/2 cup quick-cooking oats
1/4 cup toasted wheat germ
1/2 cup butter, softened
1 tbs. grated orange zest
3/4 cup packed brown sugar, divided
2 eggs
1/2 cup blanched whole almonds
1/2 cup shredded coconut

Heat oven to 350°. In a large bowl, beat flour, oats, wheat germ, butter, zest and ½ cup of the brown sugar at low speed until just mixed. Increase speed to medium (or beat with a wooden spoon) and beat for 2 minutes longer: mixture will look dry.

With lightly floured hands, shape mixture into a ball, then press firmly into an ungreased 8-inch square pan.

In a small bowl, beat eggs with remaining ¼ cup brown sugar; stir in almonds and coconut. Pour evenly over mixture in pan.

Bake for 35 minutes, or until a toothpick inserted in the center comes out clean. Cool completely in pan on a wire rack. Cut into bars.

HONEY BREAKFAST BARS

Makes 24–32 bars

These no-bake treats are a healthier version of Rice Krispie bars. If you can't find dried strawberries, use any type of dried fruit.

1 cup honey
1½ cups peanut butter
½ cup sugar
8 cups crispy rice cereal
1 cup chopped dried strawberries

Lightly grease a 9 x 13-inch pan. In a large saucepan over medium heat, bring honey, peanut butter and sugar to a boil, stirring occasionally. Stir in cereal. Mix well until coated.

Press mixture into prepared pan and refrigerate until firm. Cut into bars.

GRAPE NUTS-PEANUT BUTTER BARS

Makes 24 bars

Tahini, similar to peanut butter but made of sesame seeds, contains essential minerals, protein and unsaturated or "good" fat. Use all peanut butter if you can't find tahini.

½ cup peanut butter
½ cup tahini (sesame seed
    paste)
1 cup maple syrup

3 cups Grape Nuts cereal
1 cup dried cranberries
2 tbs. wheat germ, optional

Spray a 9 x 13-inch pan with nonstick cooking spray. In a large saucepan, mix together peanut butter and tahini until well blended. Add maple syrup and bring to a boil over medium-low heat, stirring occasionally. Remove from heat, add cereal and dried cranberries and mix thoroughly.

Spread evenly into prepared pan. Sprinkle wheat germ on top, if desired. Refrigerate until firm and cut into bars.

HIGH PROTEIN ENERGY BARS

Makes 10 bars

The protein in these bars comes from the egg whites, soymilk, protein powder and, surprisingly, the prunes, which also provide vitamin C and potassium. Nowadays prunes are often referred to as dried plums. Find protein powder in health food stores.

3 egg whites, lightly beaten
½ cup applesauce
¼ cup water
1 tsp. vanilla extract
1 cup honey
3½ cups old-fashioned oats
1½ cups dry soymilk powder
¼ cup vanilla soy protein
¼ cup wheat germ
½ cup chopped prunes

Heat oven to 325°. Spray a 9 x 13-inch pan with nonstick cooking spray.

In a medium bowl, whisk together egg whites, applesauce, water, vanilla and honey.

In a large bowl mix, together oats, dry soymilk, soy protein, wheat germ and prunes. Add applesauce mixture to oats mixture and blend with a wooden spoon until well combined. The batter will be thick.

Spread evenly into prepared pan. Bake for 15 to 20 minutes, or until lightly browned around the edges. Cool completely on a wire rack. Cut into bars.

CHEWY CINNAMON ENERGY BARS

Makes 24 bars

Like cinnamon rolls with the nutritious punch of oats, these are also a guilt-free dessert.

1 cup old-fashioned or quick-cooking oats
1/2 cup packed brown sugar
1/3 cup shredded coconut
1/3 cup butterscotch chips
1/3 cup chopped pecans
1 pkg. (17.4 oz.) cinnamon swirl quick bread & coffee cake mix
1/2 cup butter, melted
1/3 cup water
2 egg yolks

Heat oven to 375°. Grease a 9 x 13-inch pan. In a food processor workbowl, combine oats, brown sugar, coconut, butterscotch chips and pecans; process 10 seconds or until coarsely ground.

Set cinnamon swirl package from bread mix aside. In a large bowl combine bread mix and oats mixture. Stir in butter, water and egg yolks; mix well.

Spread half of batter in prepared pan. Sprinkle with cinnamon swirl from package. Drop remaining batter by spoonfuls over cinnamon swirl; carefully spread batter evenly over cinnamon mixture.

Bake for 25 to 30 minutes, or until edges are firm. Cool completely on a wire rack. Cut into bars.

CRISPY SEED HEALTH BARS

Makes 24 bars

Pumpkin seeds are loaded with minerals and antioxidants.

2 cups crispy rice cereal
2 cups old-fashioned oats
1/2 cup raisins
1/2 cup shelled roasted salted sunflower seeds
1/2 cup salted pepitas (green pumpkin seeds)

1/2 cup unsalted roasted soy nuts
1/2 cup packed brown sugar
1/2 cup light corn syrup
1/2 cup peanut butter
1/2 tsp. ground cardamom
1 tsp. vanilla extract

Spray a 9 x 13-inch pan with nonstick cooking spray. In a bowl, stir together cereal, oats, raisins, sunflower seeds, pepitas and soy nuts. In a saucepan, combine brown sugar, corn syrup and peanut butter. Cook over medium heat until mixture boils. Remove from heat; stir in cardamom and vanilla. Pour over cereal mixture; stir to combine. Press mixture into prepared pan and refrigerate until firm. Cut into bars.

TRAIL MIX BARS

Makes 12 bars

Sunflower seeds, high in vitamin B and minerals, make a complete protein when combined with peanuts or peanut butter.

3 cups crispy rice cereal
3 cups toasted oat cereal
1½ cups raisins
½ cup shelled sunflower seeds
1 cup honey

½ cup sugar
¼ tsp. ground cardamom
2 cups peanut butter
1 tsp. vanilla extract

Grease a 15 x10-inch jelly roll pan. In a large bowl, combine rice and oat cereals, raisins and sunflower seeds. Set aside. In a medium saucepan, combine honey, sugar and cardamom. Cook over medium heat until mixture comes to a boil. Boil for 1 minute. Add peanut butter and vanilla; stir until peanut butter is melted. Pour over cereal mixture; mix well. Press mixture into prepared pan. Cool completely and cut into bars.

RICE CEREAL ENERGY BARS

Makes 24 bars

*A nutritious, easy, quick peanut butter/cereal snack that kids —
and you — will gobble up.*

1/2 cup sesame seeds
1/2 cup shelled unsalted
  sunflower seeds
1/2 cup pitted chopped dates
1/2 cup raisins
1/2 cup dried apricots
1/2 cup dried cherries
1/2 cup semisweet chocolate
  chips

1 cup old-fashioned oats
7 cups crispy rice cereal
1 cup corn syrup
1 cup sugar
1 1/2 cups chunky peanut butter
1 cup dry milk powder
1 tsp. vanilla extract
1/2 tsp. almond extract

Grease a 10 x 15-inch jellyroll pan. Combine sesame seeds and sunflower seeds in a dry skillet over medium heat. Cook, stirring frequently, until fragrant and toasted. Set aside to cool.

Combine dates, raisins, apricots, cherries, chocolate chips and the toasted seeds in the workbowl of a food processor. Pulse until chopped but not a paste. Transfer to a large bowl and combine with oats and rice cereal.

In a small microwave-safe bowl, mix together corn syrup, sugar and peanut butter. Microwave on high for 1 to 2 minutes, until bubbly. Stir in dry milk powder, vanilla and almond extract.

Pour peanut butter mixture over cereal mixture and stir with a wooden spoon until everything is evenly coated. Press mixture into prepared pan using wet hands. Cool completely before cutting into bars.

CHOCOLATE COMBO TRAIL MIX BARS

Makes 24 bars

With nuts, dried fruit and chocolate, these bars have all the elements of trail mix in a portable and delicious package.

1 cup (2 sticks) unsalted butter, softened
1 cup honey, divided
1 tsp. lemon juice
2 cups whole wheat flour
1 cup quick-cooking oats
1/2 cup wheat germ
2 eggs
1 cup chopped almonds
1 cup jumbo or regular semisweet chocolate chips
1/2 cup pitted chopped dates
1/2 cup chopped dried apricots
1/2 cup unsweetened shredded coconut
2 tbs. sesame seeds

Heat oven to 350°. In a medium bowl mix together butter, ¾ cup of the honey and lemon juice until well blended.

In a separate bowl, combine flour, oats and wheat germ; stir into honey mixture until smooth. Spread evenly in an ungreased 9 x 13-inch pan. Set aside.

In a medium bowl, beat eggs while gradually pouring in remaining ¼ cup honey. Stir in almonds, chocolate chips, dates, apricots, coconut and sesame seeds until they are evenly distributed and well coated. Spread over crust in the pan.

Bake for 30 to 35 minutes, or until center is set and top is lightly browned. Cool in pan. Cool completely on a wire rack. Cut into bars.

WHITE CHOCOLATE BREAKFAST BARS

Makes 20 bars

Honey has been used for centuries as an antiseptic and a digestive aid. It contains minerals essential for good health.

2 oz. white chocolate, chopped
1½ cups honey
¼ cup (½ stick) butter
⅔ cup chunky peanut butter
1 tbs. vanilla extract

1 cup shelled sunflower seeds
½ cup wheat germ
1 cup chopped dried apricots
5 cups quick-cooking oats

In a large saucepan over medium-low heat, combine white chocolate, honey, butter and peanut butter. Cook, stirring constantly, until mixture boils; boil for 1 minute. Remove from heat and add vanilla. Stir sunflower seeds, wheat germ, apricots and oats into chocolate mixture. Pour mixture onto an ungreased cookie sheet and flatten into a large rectangle about 1 inch thick. Cool completely, then cut into bars.

SOY NUT BUTTER CEREAL BARS

Makes 24 bars

Soy nut butter is high in protein and Omega 3 fatty acids. Find it in the health food section of your grocery store.

1 cup sugar
1 cup white corn syrup
1½ cups soy nut butter or
   peanut butter

7 cups wheat flake cereal
1 cup chocolate chips
1 cup peanut butter chips

Grease a 9 x 13-inch pan. In a large saucepan, combine sugar and corn syrup. Cook over medium heat until it reaches a boil. Stir in soy nut butter until mixture is smooth. Remove from heat and stir in cereal. Pat cereal mixture into prepared pan. Melt peanut butter chips and chocolate chips together over a double boiler (or microwave on high for 1 to 2 minutes in a glass bowl). Spread melted mixture over cereal bars and refrigerate to set before cutting into bars.

CHOCOLATE FRUITY ENERGY BARS

Makes 18 bars

These sweet treats are high in antioxidants, minerals and fiber.

1 cup (2 sticks) unsalted butter, softened
1 cup honey, divided
1 tsp. lemon juice
2 cups whole wheat flour
1 cup quick-cooking oats
1/2 cup wheat germ
2 egg whites
1 cup chopped almonds
1 cup semisweet jumbo or regular chocolate chips
1/2 cup pitted chopped dates
1/2 cup chopped dried apricots
1/2 cup unsweetened shredded coconut
2 tbs. sesame seeds
1/2 cup semisweet mini chocolate chips

Heat oven to 350°. In a medium bowl, mix together butter, ¾ cup of the honey and lemon juice until well blended. In a separate bowl combine flour, oats and wheat germ. Stir into honey mixture until all ingredients are combined. Spread evenly into an ungreased 9 x 13-inch pan. Set aside.

In a large bowl, beat egg whites for 2 minutes. Gradually stir in remaining ¼ cup honey. Stir in almonds, jumbo chocolate chips, dates, apricots, coconut and sesame seeds until they are evenly mixed and well coated. Spread over crust in the pan.

Bake for 30 to 35 minutes, or until center is set and top is lightly browned. Place on a wire rack and sprinkle mini chocolate chips evenly over top of hot bars. Cool completely before cutting into bars.

COCONUT MANGO ENERGY BARS

Makes 64 bars

Decadent, chewy coconut has less fat than most nuts, and boosts your nutrition with potassium, magnesium and protein.

3 cups sweetened shredded coconut
½ cup all-purpose flour
10 oz. sweetened condensed milk (about ⅔ of a 14-oz. can)
1 cup cornflakes, crushed

2 bars (1.5 oz. each) milk chocolate with crisped rice, chopped
½ cup chopped dried mango
1½ tsp. grated orange zest

Heat oven to 350°. Grease an 8-inch square pan. In a medium bowl, combine coconut and flour. Stir in condensed milk, cornflakes, chocolate, mango and orange zest.

Spread mixture evenly into prepared pan. Bake for 25 to 30 minutes, or until golden. Cool on a wire rack. Cut into 1-inch square bars.

CHOCOLATE GRANOLA ENERGY BARS

Makes 16 bars

Nothing recharges the body and encourages tired hikers faster than a quick snack on the trail. Choose dark chocolate for the antioxidants.

1½ cups granola
½ cup Spanish peanuts
1 cup chocolate chips
½ cup dried cranberries

1 cup prunes
1 cup dried peaches
½ cup dried apricots

Line an 8-inch square pan with waxed paper. In a large bowl, combine granola, peanuts, chocolate chips and cranberries. In a food processor workbowl, combine prunes, peaches and apricots. Process until smooth, scraping down sides of workbowl a few times. Stir pureed fruit into granola mixture. Mix well. Press evenly into prepared pan. Air-dry overnight. Cut into bars.

INDEX